Robert Eggleston

D1798126

AS A BOY

Kentish Prayer

Though my feet are hewn
From Kentish clay;
Though my heart be weak
And prone to stray;
Though faith be threadbare
And nearly spent;
Though heart be torn
In one long rent;
Though mind may wander
And strength be frail;
At the end by grace
I shall not fail.
I shall not fail
Nor fail to stand
For God still holds me
In his hand.

Poems and Lyrics

Published July 2006

British Library Cataloguing-In-Publication Data
A record of this publication is available from the British Library.

ISBN 1846851610
978-1-84685-161-2

First Published July 2006 by Exposure Publishing, an imprint of Diggory Press, Three Rivers, Minions, Liskeard, Cornwall, PL14 5LE.
www.diggorypress.com

Index

Foreword by Simon Richardson,
Editor, Christian bands.

My first personal encounter with Robert's work was by having the pleasure of hearing Julie Hall's beautiful voice singing the song 'Even an Angel'. The lyrics of which are included in this book.

Beyond the angelic voice of Julie lay words that could only have been born in the heart of a man versed in the pleasures and the pain of this life. For me, becoming aware of a talent such as Robert's instantly creates intrigue, curiosity and a desire to know and read more.

Throughout this book of verse and poetry, you will be taken on a journey. It's a lyrical journey that encompasses the tears, the joy, the laughter and all of humanities' emotions. Sometimes, you may cry as you recognise within your own journey through life, instances and moments which Robert has captured eloquently in verse. At other times you may feel your spirit rising within you in ecstatic joy at the wonder of all that makes our human life and its harmony with creation and our God around us, merge.

I envisage this book becoming one of those timeless treasures which you will refer to time and time again throughout your life. Such a gift, such a talent, is one to be celebrated and cherished. I commend Robert Eggleston and 'As a Boy' to you.

Enjoy. God Bless You.

Simon Richardson

Preface

I have always considered hang gliding to be a fairly reckless activity although I must confess to a sneaking admiration for the men and women who engage in the sport. I have looked in wonder as they float above the South Downs escarpment, near my home in Sussex. I can only imagine the great sense of joy and freedom that the fliers experience as they catch a thermal and then soar above the hills and plains like great birds of prey. It must be truly awesome. I, however, lack their courage. What would concern me would be the likely ignominious and painful landing in a farmer's field below.

However, as I publish my first volume of poems and lyrics I am beginning to feel that hang gliding may be the safer activity after all. At least I would only be risking danger to the body and, if I landed badly, the mind. But publishing a book of poetry, particularly one that is rooted in that awkward thing called "faith" carries far greater risks. It exposes the deepest emotions to public display and highlights weaknesses, failings and feelings that most sane men would prefer to keep hidden. It is a truly vulnerable experience.

For those who find the expression of vulnerability in these poems at odds with the certainty of their own beliefs I would only say that I have, through this work, been deeply touched by the power and majesty of the grace, love and mercy of God. It is in the weakness of the moment that I have found God truly making himself known to me. I hope that this comes across in this book and that you are similarly touched.

Some of the poems and lyrics may strike you as sad. It is true that some have been written as a consequence of loss or regret. But I have always tried to find a hope somewhere in the circumstances that are thrown up by life (and by hope I do not mean mere wishful thinking). The three poems that take Mother Julian of Norwich's phrase, *"all will be well, all will be well and all manner of things will be well"* is a reminder of that hope.

I do not propose analysing the poems and lyrics here. This is because I would like you to draw your own conclusions about the content (although if you wanted to email me with questions I will endeavour to reply - see email address below). Also, if there is even a remote chance that, when I am dead, I become a University set text I would want to leave future generations chewing over the words and meanings without guidance from the author (it will be such good fun watching and listening)!!

One thing I will say is that you will notice that I sometimes refer to Kentish clay. I spent the first seven years of my life in Snodland, near Maidstone in Kent before moving to Brighton in 1964 (I now live in Burgess Hill, West Sussex). Kentish clay is a bit like a signature for me and it reminds me of some of my roots and it is the place of my earliest memories. Houseman was, of course, able to write extensively on Shropshire themes even though he came from Worcestershire. But I guess he was drawn to the "blue remembered hills" of his youth as I am drawn to the North Downs of mine.

I suppose also that the book starts with the childish innocence of the poem that I have used as the title to this volume and those innocent days belong to Kent.

The clay (and I have as much in Burgess Hill as I remember seeing in Kent), of course, highlights the weakness of my human condition which is made manifest in adulthood. But it is a condition that is made beautiful and strong by the grace of God (he is, after all, potter to my clay).

Poetry should, in my opinion, be read aloud (if only to annoy other people). Sometimes poems are even better when they are sung as, in my view, the music adds layers of meaning to the lines that are not always revealed by the simple spoken word. Many of the pieces in this book have actually been written in the knowledge that they will be set to music and I have therefore tried to keep these in their song format. In writing with music in mind I have been extremely fortunate in having, as a very good friend, Julie Hall, who has very sensitively arranged some of the poems onto two CDs. As Simon Richardson points out, she has a beautiful voice. **"Bluebells Rising"** and **"Days of Wine"** are two great acoustic albums of hers and I recommend them to you. They can be obtained by contacting Snowdrop Music **(*see details below)**.

The illustrations in the book have been drawn by Joe Samuel who was introduced to me by my publisher. I am very grateful to Joe for the way that he has used the drawings to add to the meaning and understanding of the poems. It is amazing how this venture has brought me into contact with people who I would not otherwise meet and through not meeting them my life would have been much poorer as a result. So thank you Joe.

Finally, I would like to thank Simon Richardson, the Editor of Christianbands (www.Christianbands.co.uk), for writing the Foreword to this book. I have never met Simon but I hope to meet him one day soon. I have admired his vision in setting up Christianbands which is an excellent showcase and resource for Christian music artists and part of the proceeds from this book will be going to support Simon Richardson's work.

Robert Eggleston

* If you want to contact me you can email me on snowdrop1.music@virgin.net. You can also email me at this address for further copies of the book or to order the CDs "Bluebells Rising" and "Days of Wine".

Find out more about Julie Hall on www.snowdropmusic.com and Christianbands on www.christianbands.co.uk

For Barbara
(1955 - 2002)
& the hope
and promise
of an Angel

The Stirrup and the Ground

I'm caught in between:

Rebellion and adoration;
Destruction and creation;

Reality and illusion;
Prophecy and delusion;

Clarity and confusion;
Paucity and profusion;

Logic and emotion;
The desert and the ocean;

The prison and the key;
The bars that keep me caged;
The hand that sets me free.

I'm caught in between:

Giving without measure;
Or self indulgent pleasure;

Profit without gain;
Or sacrifice and pain;

The sacred or profane;
The glory or the shame;

The pride before the fall;
Letting go and giving all;

The prison and the key;
The bars that keep me caged;
The hand that sets me free.

I'm weighing my dilemmas
So heavy in my hand.
I'm sifting grains of perished salt
Or piles of unwashed sand.

I'm looking for some answers
And hope these may be found,
So I may reach the mercy seat
Between the stirrup and the ground.

Beginning

A hand stretched out
And it was done.

Is this the way
The world began?

Was God so lonely
That he wrought
This single earth,
From holy thought?

That he weaved and curled
And bent and thus,
The universe
Came out of dust?

That from Kentish clay
He breathed and made
A living man
To love and save?

For at the start
There was rise and fall
And from first to last,
God saw,
And knew it all.

The Dawn

And there was evening and there
was morning - the first day
(Genesis: 1 v5)

A touch of pink
That ushers
Out the night,
Iridescent,
Aurora,
Eastern light.

A humble glow
That greets
The morning air
And the birds
Murmur,
Suddenly aware
Of dawns
Silent
Yet eventful coming.

The light grows
And bees begin
Their humming.
In fervent reverie
Insects pray,
Holy rituals
For the opening day.

As A Boy

All a man's ways seems right to
him, but the Lord weighs the heart
(Proverbs 21:2)

As a boy,
I remember
Chasing through allotments
On Saturday,
While dad turned potatoes
And dug the Kentish clay.

I remember
Playtime on slides and swings,
Their arms all thick with rust
And in summer months
Iced with Kentish dust.

I remember
Nibbling a milky bar
Back from the *'rec'*
And playing *flicks* with cards
Against a neighbour's wall,
(Winner takes all).

I remember
The sledge on Holly Hill
And the cement works
That made me ill.

I remember
The Tonibell that called
With wafers like sea shells,
Or cones, for a treat
(Once mine fell in the street).

I remember
The first long walk to school
With my friend and his mum
And falling from my bike
When I was young.

I remember,
As a boy,
Being weighed in the chill
Of the clinic's scales
And now,
As a man,
See how scales
Weigh me still.

Eternal Love

A love said though never spoken,
By age and decay never broken,
Love seen by eyes that want of sight,
Yet held in dreams throughout the night,
Yet held in dreams throughout the night.

Love heard in whispered silent tears,
Fragrant beyond the scent of years,
Love breathed without the need of air,
Ever present, everywhere,
Ever present, everywhere.

Love warmed by arms beyond embracing,
And with its hands forever tracing
Holy patterns within your soul.
Love eternal, divine and whole,
Love eternal, divine and whole.

Old Man Earth

"Listen to me, you who pursue
Righteousness and who seek the Lord:
look to the rock from which you were cut
and to the quarry from which you were hewn:
(Isaiah 51:1)

I am born and then torn
By the wind to the hills.

Now I AM
Old Man Earth
Who stands firm
By the cam stones
And loose heartings
And ancient granite rings.

I AM rock,
Dimly seeing still
The lambs
With dull, brown fleece
Graze on moorland grass.

I AM well worn stone
That rears up
In Helvellyn's arms
And watches an easing dew
Shift from fells
And tells the caws
Of circling crows.

I AM mountain
That hears crickets wake
And chant their mantra,
On the lichen
And the moss,
To butterflies

In priestly hues.

I AM walls and ways
Where Roman Legions trod,
Past rosaries
Of pearl and pink.

I AM formed.
The foundation.
Think,
Think,
Think.

Then think
Of the ground
From which you were hewn
The rock,
The dust,
And soil.

Think of the potter
With tireless hands
Who turns
And moulds
And toils

Who fashioned you
From granite grey,
Or Downland chalk,
Or sandstone, shale,
Or Kentish clay.

Who fashioned you
With hope and love
To live and breathe
And walk in truth.

Days Of Wine

There is a time for everything,
And a season for every activity under heaven:
(Ecclesiastes 3:1)

Days of wine;
Days of rain;
Days of glory;
Days of shame.

Days when your mouth
Is as dry as dust.
Days when you're
Searching for the lost.

Days of silence;
Days of noise;
Harassed days
Without grace or poise.

Days of joy
Of dance and song;
Days of grief
That last too long.

Days of soaring;
Days of failing;
Warm summer days
Then winter,
Cold and ailing.

Beginning days
That know no end
And ember days
That are no friend.

Days when hope
Is stripped away;
Days when hope
Is found again.

And found or not
You are in our days;
Each passing moment
Each breath, each phrase,
Each beat, each pulse
In every part,
So come dear friend
And rule my heart.

Only My Maker

O Lord, you have searched me
and you know me. You know when
I sit and when I rise;
you perceive my thoughts from afar.
You discern my going out
and my lying down;
you are familiar with all my ways.
(Psalm 139 v 1-3)

Only my maker knows
The truth behind my eyes;
The story in my heart;
The compromising lies.

Only my maker knows
The joy inside my head;
And tears I've wept at night
For dreams that I have shed.

For he knows everything
There is to know about me
He sees my thoughts from afar,

He knows all the passion
And the pleading,
All the sighing
And the bleeding
Of my heart,
He knows it all,
He sees it all.

Only my maker sees
Beneath my thin disguise
To all that I must own
Before my soul will rise.

For he knows everything
There is to know about me
He sees my thoughts from afar

He knows all the failures
And the yearning,
All the searching
And the turning
Of my heart,
He knows it all,
He sees it all.

And I will only know
His beauty born by grace
When my life rests in Him,
My heart's his dwelling place.

On The Edge

On the edge of reason,
On the edge of faith,
Need a little learning
I'm searching for your face.

I'm trying none too hard now,
I'm trying not to fold,
Uncovering all the emptiness
Whilst looking for the gold.

I'm seeking
But am I finding?
I yearn for you to come,
To take away my heart of stone
And fill me with your Son.

On the edge of darkness,
On the edge of light,
Need a little guidance
To show me what is right.

I try to catch a rainbow,
Or try to catch the sun,
Are the patterns of my future
Shaped by the race I've run?

I'm seeking
But am I finding?
I yearn for you to come,
To take away my heart of stone
And fill me with your Son.

Colours Of Life

It's the deep full rose,
Held in your lover's hand,
Or cold spattered blood
On ochre coloured land.

It's in the last dawn's
Yawning and warning fire,
Or the sudden mist
From the crowd's raging ire.

It's wave weaving blades
Kissing the still chilled earth,
Or the gnawing pain
Of envy's bitter birth.

It's the pastel shades
Of gentle, tender spring,
Or the raging lust
Of summer's casual fling.

It's the juice stained robes
And syrah tainted walls.
It's port on the lips
Of rich and greasy fools.

It's the humble earth,
The meek and serving soil.
It's the pious man
Of faith and prayer and toil.

It's Friday at noon
With crow clawed, scowling skies.
It's the lonely rage
And mascara streaked eyes.

It's the linen sheet,
As pure as any dove.
It's the God of peace
Of hope and grace and love.

It's embroidered life,
Each warp and weft and hue
It's the choice you make
"So what colours are you?"

All In This Holy Place

"Without faith, nothing is possible.
With it, nothing is impossible."
(Mary McLeod Bethune)

All in this holy place,
Where the land meets the sea and sky,
Where all the things
That cannot be
Are made possible by and by.

All in this holy place,
All in this holy place.

Not the highest,
nor the lowest;
Not the strongest,
nor the weakest;
Not the greatest,
nor the smallest;
Deserves your love
Or deserves your kind embrace.

Not the wisest,
nor the simplest;
Not the richest,
nor the poorest;
Not the most stained,
nor the purest;
Deserves your love
Or deserves to see your face.

But you freely give your heart
To ease our souls with your sure care,
And you freely give your hand
To tend the broken spirits here,
And you freely pour out grace

To bring us hope, all in this holy place.

All in this holy place,
Where the land meets the sea and sky,
Where all the things
That cannot be
Are made possible by and by.
All in this holy place,
Where God pours out his grace.

Even An Angel

The crystal lies broken,
There's a stain on the floor
And my tear streaked face
Says, we've been here before,
With sad lamentations
And brooding Amens,
Has love died between us?
Well that just depends...

For even an angel can break a wing,
And sometimes in life
The sky caves in.
And even wise men can stumble and fall,
And one day you'll realise
You know nothing
About me at all.

Illusions are shattered,
Our dreams are all spent,
Bitter words pass between us
Spun with harsh intent.
Gone are our promises
And barren that vow
Has love died between us?
Well answer me now!

For even an angel can break a wing,
And sometimes in life
The sky caves in.
And even wise men can stumble and fall,
And one day you'll realise
You know nothing
About me at all.

And how I laugh inside
Each time you say,
"Never let the sun go down
On a row".

And how I cry inside
Each time you say,
"A gentle word turns away wrath".
But I really want to hear you say...

I know that an angel can break a wing,
That sometimes in life
The sky caves in.
I know that wise men can stumble and fall,
And at last I realise
I knew nothing, I knew nothing,
I knew nothing
About you at all.

Revelations of Divine Love

"But all will be well,
and all will be well,
and all manner of things will be well"
(Mother Julian of Norwich)

In contrast to the poem "Even An Angel" which deals with the frailty of human love, the next three focus on the power of the divine love of God and the hopefulness that that love brings.

The poems all have a central phrase which has been taken from the writings of Mother Julian of Norwich, an Anchorite (recluse) living in the late fourteenth century. As a recluse Julian lived and meditated on the life of Christ and experienced her revelations on the Passion which were then set down in writing in the Revelations of Divine Love (thus becoming the first woman to write a book in England - the revelations took place in 1373).

Julian's revelations were along fairly predictable lines dealing with themes such as the love of God, the Passion, prayer and sin. What probably gives them a constant freshness is the simplicity and hopefulness in which the themes are expressed. The quotation above, which reappears in the following poems, is found in Chapter 27 in the context of sin and the pain it causes. But in this passage it is sin that points Julian to the Passion and the transformation that the Passion can have over our lives and the cleansing it brings. "It is true," she writes, "that sin is the cause of all this pain, but all will be well, and all will be well, and all manner of things will be well."

All Will Be Well

Wait for me silently
Through the lonely winter nights.
For even though the earth
Is still and cold,
It is only sleeping.

And if I am dreaming too
I still have you in my keeping.

Wait for me patiently
In the cruel and icy storm.
For even though the wind
May cut and roar,
The earth is only aching.

And if I am weeping now
It's because my heart is breaking.

But I will find you;
In the bitter
Icy wind;
In the loneliness
Of tears;
In the silence
Of the earth;
And the dreams
Of many years.

I will find you.
For my promise will come true:
That all will be well,
All will be well,
All will be well
With you.

When The Snowdrops Bloom

When the Snowdrops bloom
And a wintry sun softly
Warms your hungry soul;
That's when your heart
Will start to beat
To the rhythm
Of the gentle hope of spring.

Then I'll come to you
And will place your hand in mine.
And again you'll know
That I'm your loving friend;
I'm your heart's desire;
And your patient guide
Who's still walking
By your side.

So now lift your voice,
And banish sad imaginings.
Now lift your voice
And feel the hope that this day brings;
Now lift your voice
And boldly and joyfully sing:

"All manner of things will be well,
Will be well.
All manner of things will be well
When the Snowdrops bloom,
Deep inside my soul,
All manner of things will be well."

Bluebells Rising

To bestow on them a crown of beauty instead of ashes,
The oil of gladness instead of mourning
And a garment of praise instead of a spirit of despair
(Isaiah 61:3)

Where is the garment of praise?
The crown of beauty where?
Where is the oil of gladness
To ease the pain that I bear?

I have ashes in my hands
And a spirit cloaked with grief.
My heart, despite spring's promise of hope,
Still sings, without relief;
A song of winter's mourning.

So where will I wander now?
To the hills, the woods or streams?
My soul, it yearns for comfort and peace
But sings of stolen dreams;
A song that has no ending.

To the hills I vainly go
Where birds cry their sad refrain.
My spirit suffers still
And eyes cannot retain
Tears that are ever falling.

By still streams I walked alone
For to seek some comfort there.
The water chills my breaking heart
I stay in deep despair;
And for the forest longing.

Years I walked in search of peace,
Until to the trees I came.
There by leaf, by agèd bark
A friend called out my name;
And to my soul was whispering.

Words of comfort on my life
By him were offered there
And burdens I'd long carried
This friend he chose to bear;
To still my heart from aching.

Bluebells rising round my feet,
Garments made for glory.
Heady perfume from the dew
Brought hope to this life's story;
And joy afresh beginning.

I had ashes in my hands,
But what did the forest tell?
That at the bluebells rising
All is and all will be well;
Heart, soul and spirit healing.

Here is the garment of praise,
The crown of beauty's here,
And here is the oil of gladness
That heals the pain that you bear.

The Weaver

The sable mantle drops
Its drapes on jet black streets,
Cold, cracked and fallow fields,
And meadows, woods and hills.

A rising moon glances
Across the hardening frost
And dances with shadows
Hiding a glimpse of fox
And swooping, howling owl.

All nature, with bated
And expectant breath waits,
And waits while the world turns,
And waits as two watchers
Ponder this passing night.

They beat old arms to bear
A crisp and bitter cold
And chime with panting breath
A simple common song
That lifts and falls in pleats,
And lulls a world in sleep.

Patient Anna,
With your steely hair,
And old Simeon,
With your slate grey eyes,
Intone again and sing
Your simple slow refrain:

"Lord grant our humble hymn,
Raise up from David's stem,
A light, a hope, a prince for men."

And now the watchers wait.
They wait while the world turns;
Wait by the temple door;
And wait as incense ash
Falls cold to the floor.

They wait whilst the red fox
And the white preying owl
Find rest in hole or nest.
They wait while lambs shelter
And their shepherds shiver
In lonely hillside fold.

The Heavenly Weaver
Has seen and heard it all
And weaves his holy seams
From plain and panting threads.

He weaves while the world turns:
Weaves for the fallen man;
For saints in humble prayer;
The shepherds in their fold;
The fox in hungry lair.

He weaves from stable door
Across the sable night
A stream of sapphire stars
That heralds in the light.
He weaves his hope, his peace for men,
He weaves the Christ in Bethlehem.

The Gambler's Chance

For our struggle is not against flesh
and blood, but against the rulers,
the authorities, against the powers of
this dark world and against the spiritual
forces of evil in the heavenly realms.
(Ephesians 6:12)

"Poker ...
Blackjack....
Craps.....
Roulette.....
No tricks or traps.
Just spin the wheel

Or the barrel perhaps
Of a gun.
Come on...... Come on.......
It's just a bit of
fun.....
Dance to my tune
And then.........

When your life becomes my dance
There's always the Gambler's Chance."

I'm drowning by the green baize,
Sucking in the smoky haze,
Drinking cups of empty days,
Dying as the croupier
Twists and turns and spins
My life away.

But didn't you say
I'm free to choose,
Free to walk away
Or free to stay

And then to lose,
Simply lose it all!

Working with a loaded pack.
He's 'King high' and I've a Jack.
Cash and sweat pours off my back
And as the dealer reels me in,
Well, it's sink or swim,
It's win or bust.

But if all seems lost
I'm still free to stand
Free to take the ground
And hold the hand
Hold the hand of life!

Now all that's left is one last bet.
One last bid to pay my debt.
"Stake your life," the game's now set
And the dealer turns the cards,
Then laughs and sneers and grins
And, mocking, wins.

"You hoped to win this game",
He simply sings,
"Or somehow save your life.
With a simple spin of the wheel;
Or the gentle roll of a dice;
An easy turn of a card;
Or a bullet from a gun;
But it doesn't matter now
How they fall, roll or run
For you're dancing to my tune
And I've made your life my dance
So come on, come on, come on
Come take the Gambler's Chance."

And now that the final hand's been played
And all that I had has been unmade,
And too many words are left unsaid,
And too many hopes are left for dead,

I need to know,
Need to hear you say
That it's still not too late,
That I can walk away.
It's not too late
To make a stand
To take the ground
And hold the hand
Hold the hand of life?

For Voices

Led like a lamb,
> *(to be wounded for us.)*

Just like a lamb,
> *(a lamb to the slaughter.)*

O Holy one,
> *(the Son of God.)*

Jesus betrayed by a man.
> *(Jesus – victorious.)*

> They whipped his back.
> But then he said,
> No lash will forever mar me.

>> They nailed him there.
>> But then he said,
>> No tree will forever hold me.

> They pierced his side.
> But then he said,
> No spear will forever bruise me.

>> They mocked his life.
>> But then he said,
>> No words will forever harm me.

> They buried him.
> But then he said,
> I've risen come and glorify me.

I've risen come and glorify me
I've risen come and glorify me

My Lord's Love For Me

Older than the oldest oak tree
And deeper than the deepest sea,
Infinite like the stars of heaven
Is my Lord's love for me.

Clearer than the clear blue water,
More graceful than a bird in flight,
Rising above the highest mountain
Is my Lord's love for me.

For this is perfect love
A love so wide and long
And high and deep.
This is perfect love
And through your love
My life is made complete

Brighter than a summer's rainbow,
More perfumed than the new mown hay,
A precious jewel beyond all measure
Is my Lord's love for me.

For this is perfect love
A love so wide and long
And high and deep.
This is perfect love
And through your love
My life is made complete

The Cross That Set Me Free

I'm lost in wonder,
By the spaces in between,
In the silence and simplicity,
In the seen and great unseen.

I'm drowned in worship,
In the phrases and the rhymes,
In the heavy hearted melodies,
In your seasons and your times.

I'm held by your love,
By your pure unguarded grace,
By your mercies pouring down on me,
By your holy heart's embrace.

I'm bound by your truth,
By the searching then the found,
In the words that raise or frighten me,
In your perfect solid ground.

I'm moved by your hope,
In my penance and my praise,
In uncomplicated certainties,
In my firm or fragile ways.

I trust in your life,
In the sacrifice for me,
In the glory, pain and suffering,
In the cross that set me free.

I Am In The Stream

May the Spirit satisfy you
with the water of grace
(Carmina Gadelica)

I am in the stream
And see the grey cloth on dull hills.
Its fine threads fall
Like frail, drab drapes
Through coarse crack and crevice.

*And the rain whispered
"I am the stream."*

Then a spring arose
In silence
On the waking earth.
So that col became a mother
And nursed the gentle stream.

*And the spring whispered
"I am the stream."*

Water trickled across
Some tickled stones
And called with a
Click,
Clack,
Clatter

To chattering cousins
Who joined a glittering wake.
It fed from
Cwm and corrie,
Tarn and burn
And raced with glee
Past rocks and scree

And played its foam
On praying
Fern and reed.

And the foam whispered,
"From the mists that dust
The distant hills
To the timbrels
Of the water's rush,
I am the stream.
I flow to give you life
And I am in the stream."

Paragraph Of Praise

"Will you give me a paragraph of praise?
Because today, *'it's nice'* is not enough.
And can I have more than an 'auntie's kiss'?
I long for the bliss of a lover's touch.

And fill me a glass right up to the brim
For meagre portions will never suffice.
While you're at it, throw a party or two,
Invite all our friends - now that would be nice!

Will you give me a paragraph of praise?
Give me your heart whilst it's still beating true?
Let both of your arms embrace my poor world.
Show me some passion in all that you do.

There's a barn in the field longing for grain;
There's a wide river bed praying for rain;
Bellies are empty and begging for food;
Souls will weigh heavy apart from the rood.

Called To Serve

I've lent my weight to the oaken plough
And turned my face to the westron wind.
These forty years, by my weathered hand,
I've moved the blade and carved the land.

Under Wedgwood blue and lowering skies,
In last bright frosts and gathering storms,
From the dawning light to the ember day
I've shaped the unwieldy Kentish clay.

From corner copse to the open brow,
With starlings, ravens and crows in tow,
From flatlands plains to the downland steep
I've ploughed my furrows both straight and deep.

Cut straight and deep with my gentle team,
Whose brasses shone and fetlocks steamed
Who bore the scars of our honest toil
As we worked and moved the heavy soil.

But I've never seen the flowers bloom
Nor seen the corn gathered to the barn
Yet still I strained my every nerve
And laboured on, I was called to serve.

I was called to serve and never yield,
Not quit the toil of my Master's field
But to humbly work both night and day
And journey on in my Master's way.

Let Me Be Free

Don't stifle me.
Don't fence me in.
Oh please
Let me be me
And let me be free:

To ride with the black, wild horses
If I want to;
And chase the foam into the sea;
Beckon the rain
From the storm clouds;
And watch lightning from under a tree.
Oh, oh, oh just let me be free!

Don't harness me.
Don't lock me up.
Oh please
Let me be me
And let me be free:

To swim in the surging rivers
If I want to;
And fly like an eagle turned free;
Go near the edge
Of a mountain;
And roll down the hills recklessly.
Oh, oh, oh just let me be free!

Don't stifle me.
Don't fence me in.
Oh please
Let me be me
And let me be free,

To sleep in a field with the stars
If I want to;
Run naked down to the sea;
Withstand the heat
Of the desert;
And shout till my spirit bursts free...

"Let me make my mistakes
Before my heart breaks
And all life is emptied from me.
Oh, oh, oh let me,
Be me,
And let me be free".

Monday Again

Just wishing it was
Monday again.........

I'm sitting here
With a chipped cup
And dirty spoon,
Drinking coffee
On a Wednesday
Just before noon.

It's weak and warm.
One long latte
Without laughter,
And then after
I've drained my dregs
I drag my eyes
To clumsy gulls
Drumming the steps,
As they pull strips
Off stale, cold chips.

My memory
Fails to fail me.
I can't forget.
Nor can old men
And their ladies
Sitting, wind swept,
On bored benches,
Or in deck chairs
In hollowed out
Pebbled trenches.

They can't forget.
They just recount
The days they've lost
With sore laments.
Nothing makes sense.

So now I plough
Through dull, tarmac
Black promenade
*(Even if the rain
Is falling hard).*

And when I must
I thrust my feet
In full, brackish
Sea filled puddles.
Head down, eyes down,
Worn and troubled
By the soaking wet
That pours through pores
And draws the flesh
Into a raw
And wrinkled mess.

*Just wishing it was
Monday again..........*

Stumbling along
Long alleyways,
Without pausing
To catch my breath,
And climbing hills,
I leave the sea
To its black moods
And clumsy gulls.

Then from the skies,
False diamonds fall
And sting my eyes
And stain the streets
In grimy tears.
Then, full of fears
I turn the key
And reach the stairs.

But is this home?
This bare board house,
This no rest house,
This lacklustre,
Weary Wednesday
Worst house, that's dull
And damp and cramped.

Or is this hell?
Where sorrows lay,
And all is grief.
Where hope is gone
Or, passing, brief.

Yes, this is hell
A hollowed out
And barren life,
An empty shell.

Memories call:
Angels hover;
The music plays;
A wintry sun
Recalls the days
When all was well
And well my soul.

But now I sit
Beyond the pale,
Behind the glass,
Outside the veil,
And wait and wait
And wait in vain
For pleasing rhymes
And days of wine,
And hope again.

I wont forget
That life I knew,
And all the joy
I knew in you.

I wont forget
That angel face,
That soul, that heart,
That long embrace.

I wont forget
Yet can but dream
Of all the things
That might have been.

And in those dreams
I see you there
My doe eyed girl
With blessèd hair.

Just wishing it was
Monday again........

I'm sitting here
With a chipped cup
And dirty spoon

Drinking coffee
On a Wednesday
Just before noon.
Just wishing it was
Monday.........
soon......

Always

Where can I go to find you?
Or must I wander still?

Run to me through the summer fields
As the soft grass caresses you.

Where can I go to find you?
Or must I walk away?

Bathe with me in the mountain streams
As pure water refreshes you.

Where can I go to find you?
Or must I be alone?

Climb to me on the highest peaks
As a gentle breeze kisses you.

For I will always have you in my heart
Deep down you know,
Deep down you know that:

You and I will never part
Deep down you know,
Deep down you know that.
For I will always have you in my heart.

Where can I go to find you?
Or must I sleep until you come?

Sink down to me in the ocean deep
As heavy seas try to drown you.

Where can I go to find you?
Or just dream of your lovely face?

Wait for me in the barren wastes
As an emptiness surrounds you.

For I will always have you in my heart
Deep down you know,
Deep down you know that:

You and I will never part
Deep down you know,
Deep down you know that
I will always have you in my heart.

Sign Of The Times

Everyone's looking for signs,
Everyone's looking for wonders.
Are the rooks nesting high?
Is there dew on the fleece?

Everyone's reading the runes
To find their lottery numbers,
Hoping for salvation
But never finding peace.

Everyone's watching the wind,
Trusting in the wheel of fortune,
Life lived in the fast lane
And shaking hands with fate.

Everyone's losing the day,
Are frozen in the headlights,
Think they'll catch the last boat
Although the hour's late.

And though the people say:
That lightning never strikes twice.
The writing's on the wall
Will you read its sweet advice?
Maranatha.

It's the sign of the times,
Maranatha.
It's the sign of the times,
Jesus on the road.

Unfailing

I will love you the same.
Though the stars melt into the sea;
Though the flowers lose their bloom;
Though age grips you and greys you;
I will love you the same.

I will love you the same.
Through all your uncertainties;
Or your anxious agonies;
Though your heart's heavy burdened;
I will love you the same.

I will love you the same.
For your wholeness and oneness;
For your essence and difference;
For all seasons and all time;
I will love you the same.

I will love you the same.
In your weakness and wanderings;
In your dreaming and searching;
In your giving and taking;
I will love you the same.

I will love you the same.
With tenderness and passion;
With my richness and fullness;
With everlasting favour;
I will love you the same.

I will love you the same.

Too Long In Babylon

In the years of our captivity,
We mourned for the harps hanging
From the trees;
So many songs were failing
And spirits ailing.

In the years of our captivity,
We sat in our lonely rooms
In the night;
With only silence playing
And shadows dancing.

In the years of our captivity,
We didn't play on the harp
By the shore,
Or kiss its golden strings
On the rolling moor.

In the years of our captivity
We washed tender, fragile dreams
In the streams;
And then left them there to dry
But never to die.

We have lived too long in Babylon
But now it's time to travel on,
And find our plot, our space, our peace
That we can call our own Zion.

Leave It All Behind

But those who hope in the Lord will renew
their strength. They will soar on wings like eagles;
they will run and not grow weary, they will walk
and not be faint.
(Isaiah 40:31)

I'm going to leave it all behind,
All the heartache and the pain.
Going to lie down by your side,
'Til you lift me up again.

I'm going to leave it all behind,
All the bitterness and gall.
Going to rest in gentle arms,
Trust in him who sees it all.

And it will not be
A stranger's hand
That will lift me up,
That will dust me down
And set me on my feet.

No, it will not be
A stranger's hand
That renews my strength,
So that I can run
And soar with Eagle's wings.

I'm going to leave it all behind
And walk gently with my friend.
We'll walk humbly hand in hand
In a hope that knows no end.

Reminders

The evening star,
Sun on the water,
The deer's most graceful leap.

White doves flying,
Harvest moon rising,
The white capped mountain peak.

Though words may fail
And man may fall
Creation still recalls
Your hand is in it all.

The moorland's scent,
The gulls' clear crying,
Trout glistening in the lake.

Crisp snow falling,
On tree tops hanging,
Skies clearing when I wake.

Though words may fail
And man may fall
Creation still recalls
Your hand is in it all.

Hawks soaring,
The sun's slow setting,
Hares running in the mist.

Larks hovering
With Thrushes singing,
Their voices heaven blest.

Though words may fail
And man may fall
Creation still recalls
Your hand is in it all.

Kentish Prayer

Though my feet are hewn
From Kentish clay;

Though my heart be weak
And prone to stray;

Though faith be threadbare
And nearly spent;

Though heart be torn
In one long rent;

Though mind may wander
And strength be frail;

At the end by grace
I shall not fail.

I shall not fail
Nor fail to stand
For God still holds me
In his hand.

He Will Give

He will give you
Flowers in the desert;
The aching tears of grief;
Meaning from the rainfall;
Joy beyond belief.

He will give you
Spirit on the mountain;
Hope along the way;
Laughter in the storm clouds;
Light for your darkest day.

He will give you
Peace when you least expect it;
Rest when your toil is done;
Abundance when you're empty;
Heaven when the race is won.

Agape

Agape,
Agape,
Agape,
Agape.

There is no truth,
There is no word,
There is no sound,
There is no breath,

That can reach into my heart,
Like the promise that you made,
Right from the very start.

Agape,
Agape,
Agape.

Epitaph

This is for you,
For I have gone
And left this place
That once was hearth and home.

I'll walk no more,
Nor stray, nor roam
On northern hills,
Or on the downland turf.

I will not kick
The Kentish Clay
Or wipe its dust
From playtime slide or swing.

But in its bed
I'll quiet lay
And wait on him
Who's known my heart each day.

And if I may
I have one hope,
One last request:

That I may live
with my Angel
At my breast,
And in that hope
I'll find eternal rest.